LIGHTNING BOLT BOOKS™

Motorcycles
on the Move

Lee Sullivan Hill

Lerner Publications Company
Minneapolis

To my friend Susan
with thanks for all
her help and many
mugs of coffee

Lerner Publications Company
A division of Lerner Publishing Group, Inc.
241 First Avenue North
Minneapolis, MN 55401 U.S.A.

Website address: www.lernerbooks.com

Library of Congress Cataloging-in-Publication Data

Hill, Lee Sullivan, 1958–
      Motorcycles on the Move / by Lee Sullivan Hill.
          p.   cm. — (Lightning bolt books ™— Vroom-vroom)
      Includes index.
      ISBN 978–0–7613–6026–1 (lib. bdg. : alk. paper)
      1. Motorcycles—Juvenile literature. I. Title.
   TL440.15.H5523 2011
      629.227'5—dc22   2009043792

Manufactured in the United States of America
1 — CG — 12/15/10

Contents

Cycle Variety

Motorcycles zoom on two wheels.
How fast do they go?

This rider does a wheelie while practicing for a race.

Superbikes go superfast. They go more than 200 miles (322 kilometers) per hour!

5

Do you see the superbike racer lean into the turn? **His knee almost touches the ground!**

Look how close to the track this racer is!

Dirt bikes race
through dirt
and mud.

Dirt bikes have bumpy tires.
Bumpy tires grip the dirt track.

These tires help keep riders from wiping out.

Street bikes are not made for racing.
But street bikes can lead the parade!

Cycle Control and Safety

A driver controls the motorcycle.

Sometimes there's room for a rider. Both driver and rider wear helmets. Helmets protect heads in a crash.

Don't forget your helmet if you're going for a ride.

Leather clothes also protect the rider and the driver. Leather won't rip in a fall.

A windshield protects the driver from wind and bugs.

13

How They Work

Ready to go? Almost!
How do you start this thing?

Just turn a key and push
a button. VROOM! The
motorcycle starts.

A biker starts his
motorcycle's engine.

An engine makes the motorcycle go.

Most motorcycle engines are on the outside of the bike.

Motorcycles run on gas like a car. The gas tank is above the engine.

This is the motorcycle's gas tank.

The engine turns the rear wheel. The rear wheel moves the motorcycle.

The front wheel leads the way.
The driver turns the handlebars
to steer.

The throttle is on the handlebars. The throttle controls the engine.

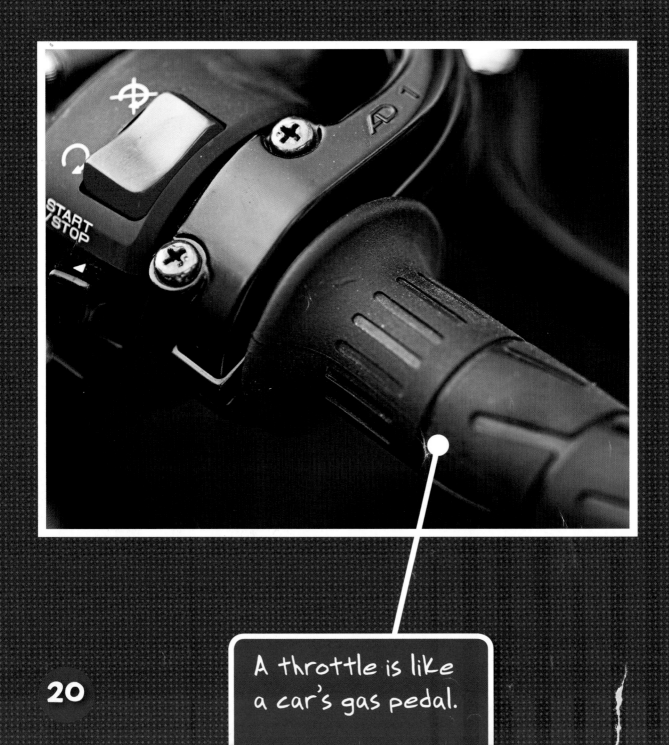

A throttle is like a car's gas pedal.

The driver twists the throttle to go fast or slow.

The brake lever is on the handlebars too. The driver squeezes the brake lever to slow down and stop.

All done?
A kickstand
holds up the
motorcycle.
The motorcycle
will be ready for
your next trip.

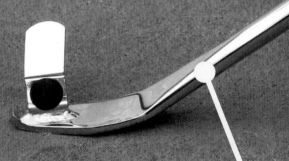

This kickstand looks
similar to a kickstand
on a bicycle.

Cycle Travel

Ready for another ride?
Touring motorcycles go fast and far.

Touring motorcycles have soft seats. Soft seats are good for long rides.

These cushy seats help riders feel comfortable when they are traveling.

Luggage holds food and
clothes for the trip.
What will you pack?

These riders' extra clothes
are secure in the back.

The rider is ready for a trip.

But hey! Where's the driver?

Motorcycle Diagrams

street bike

dirt bike

superbike

touring bike

Fun Facts

- The first gas-powered motorcycle was built in 1885. It could go only 12 miles (19 km) per hour.

- The Harley-Davidson Motor Company is the oldest motorcycle maker in the world. It was founded in 1903 in Milwaukee, Wisconsin.

- The first motorcycle factory was in Munich, Germany. It opened in 1894.

- The fastest racing motorcycles can go more than 200 miles (322 km) per hour.

- Some motorcycle riders and drivers wear yellow rain gear called banana suits. The banana suits keep people from getting soaked in wet weather.

Glossary

brake lever: a lever that a driver squeezes to make the brakes slow down the motorcycle

dirt bike: a motorcycle made for driving in dirt and mud

engine: the machine that powers a motorcycle. Most motorcycle engines run on gas.

street bike: a motorcycle that is built for driving on streets and highways

superbike: a superfast racing motorcycle

throttle: the part that controls the engine and makes the motorcycle go faster or slower

touring motorcycle: a motorcycle that is built for long rides. Touring motorcycles usually have soft seats and luggage.

Further Reading

Brecke, Nicole, and Patricia M. Stockland. *Cars, Trucks, and Motorcycles You Can Draw*. Minneapolis: Millbrook Press, 2010.

Enchanted Learning: Vehicle Online Coloring Pages http://www.enchantedlearning.com/vehicles/paintonline.shtml

Goodman, Susan E. *Motorcycles!* New York: Random House, 2007.

Roberts, Cynthia. *Motorcycles*. Chanhassen, MN: Child's World, 2007.

Zobel, Derek. *Motorcycles*. Minneapolis: Bellwether Media, 2010.

Index

Photo Acknowledgments

The images in this book are used with the permission of: © Goce Risteski/Dreamstime.com, p. 2; © Fckncg/Dreamstime.com, p. 3; © Cdonofrio/Dreamstime.com, p. 4; © Ahmad Faizal Yahya/Dreamstime.com, p. 5; © TENGKU BAHAR/AFP/Getty Images, p. 6; © Joe McBride/Taxi/Getty Images, p. 7; © Dave Blackey/All Canada Photos/CORBIS, p. 8; © Justin Sullivan/Getty Images, p. 9; © Flirt/SuperStock, p. 10; © TRANSTOCK, pp. 11, 18, 21 © Thinkstock/Comstock Images/Getty Images, p. 12; © Steve Mason/Photodisc/Getty Images, p. 13; © Kenneth Sponsler/Dreamstime.com, p. 14; © Miguel Sobreira/Alamy, p. 15; © Alexandru Ionescu/Dreamstime.com, p. 16; © Anthony Berenyi/Dreamstime.com, p. 17; © All Canada Photos/SuperStock, p. 19; © Michael Soo/Alamy, p. 20; © David Muscroft/SuperStock, p. 22; © Digito!!/Dreamstime.com, p. 23; © www.gerardbrown.co.uk/Alamy, pp. 24, 26; © imagebroker/Alamy, p. 25; © BLOOMimage/Getty Images, p. 27; © Laura Westlund/Independent Picture Service, p. 28; © Dave King/Dorling Kindersley/Getty Images, p. 29; © Susan Leggett/Dreamstime.com, p. 30; © Avesun/Dreamstime.com, p. 31.

Front cover: © Julián Rovagnati/Dreamstime.com (top); © Mlan61/Dreamstime.com (bottom).